CH00409055

Delectable Date Night

Dishes for 2

Recipes to Bring Your Love to Life!

BY: ROSE RIVERA

© 2021 Rose Rivera All Rights Reserved

———— ···· ✳ ···· ————

A Book Copyright Page

All rights are reserved for this book. On no account you are allowed to copy, print, publish, sell or make any kind of change to this book. Only the author has this permission. In case you have a copied version of this book please delete it and get the original one. It will support the author and he will be able to make even more helpful and fun cookbooks.

Make sure that you take every step with caution when you follow the instruction in this book. It's a book with information that was doubled checked by the author but you are responsible for your own actions and decisions.

Table of Contents

Introduction 6

Date night for 2 sometimes lasts till the next morning… Here are some breakfasts to share…...... 8

   1 – Coconut Lime Smoothie Bowls 9

   2 – Easy Cheesy Breakfast Quiche for 2 11

   3 – Eggs Lorraine 13

   4 – Breakfast Quesadillas for 2 15

   5 – Broiled Grapefruit Breakfast 17

There are so many unique and delightful dishes you can prepare for a date night for 2. Here are some of the best….. 19

   6 – Stir Fry Scallops for 2.. 20

   7 – Cilantro Sausage with Cauliflower Lime Rice 22

   8 – Pork Chops & Rhubarb for 2 24

   9 – Shrimp & Lettuce Wraps 26

   10 – Homemade Taco Salad for 2 29

   11 – Chicken & Spinach with Parmesan Sauce............................ 31

   12 – BBQ Tropical Chicken for 2.. 33

13 – Salmon Teriyaki Bowl 36

14 – Stuffed Bell Peppers for 2 39

15 – Noodle & Spring Roll Salad 41

16 – Steak Salad with Fries for 2 43

17 – Chicken & Dumplings 45

18 – Turkey Stir Fry for 2 48

19 – Flatbread Veggie Pizza 50

20 – Spicy Enchiladas for 2 52

21 – Creamy Parmesan Tomato Soup 54

22 – Curried Chicken for 2 57

23 – Asparagus & Lemon Chicken Pasta 60

24 – Tilapia for 2 63

25 – Sage & Lemon Ricotta Gnudi 65

End your evening date for 2 with a dessert specially made for 2… 68

26 – Crème Brulee with White Chocolate 69

27 – Strawberries Romanov for 2 71

28 – Turtle Cheesecake for 2 73

29 – Bananas Foster 75

30 – Coconut Pie with Meringue for 2 77

Conclusion 80

Author Biography 81

Thank You! 82

Introduction

What types of home-made dishes are most enjoyable for date night?

Will they be simple to prepare together?

Are the necessary ingredients fairly easy to find?

Most people prefer the taste of home cooked meals, and you and your date can easily prepare one together, even if neither of you are well-versed in cooking. When you cook at home, you save money, and you can create a special ambience when the 2 of you have prepared the meal you're enjoying.

Cooking at home is more interesting when you're doing it with your significant other. It won't be mundane or boring, like pulling together breakfast or lunch for people on the go, both adults and children.

Using the recipes in this cookbook, you'll have a great shot at finding most ingredients in your home already, so you won't have to tackle a long grocery list. Shopping for food is not usually an enjoyable endeavor. But when you put your heads together and shop with one another, you can make it a quicker trip.

Check out the special date night recipes in the cookbook. Read on and learn more!

Date night for 2 sometimes lasts till the next morning... Here are some breakfasts to share...

1 – Coconut Lime Smoothie Bowls

These smoothie bowls are easy to make alone or with that special someone. The coconut and lime make them a refreshing breakfast treat.

Makes 2 Servings

Cooking + Prep Time: 20 minutes

Ingredients:

- 1 peeled, frozen banana, medium
- 1 cup of baby spinach, fresh
- 1/2 cup of cubed ice
- 1/2 cup of cubed pineapple, fresh
- 1/2 cup of peeled, cubed mango
- 1/2 cup of yogurt, Greek, plain
- 1/4 cup of coconut, shredded, sweetened
- 3 tbsp. of honey, pure
- 2 tsp. of lime zest, grated, fresh
- 1 tsp. of lime juice, fresh
- 1/2 tsp. of vanilla extract, pure

Optional: 1 tbsp. of cream cheese, spreadable

Optional toppings: extra coconut, chocolate chips, granola, sliced almonds, banana slices, lime wedges

Instructions:

Place first 11 listed ingredients in food processor. Add the cream cheese, if using. Cover. Process till you have a smooth consistency. Pour in individual bowls and serve promptly with desired toppings.

2 – Easy Cheesy Breakfast Quiche for 2

This breakfast quiche is served in a mug and makes breakfast together easy to prepare. Using the microwave makes it a delicious and fast morning meal.

Makes 1 Serving to Share

Cooking + Prep Time: 10 minutes

Ingredients:

- 1/2 cup of packed spinach, frozen/thawed
- 1 egg, large
- 1/3 cup of milk, 2%
- 1/3 cup of cheddar cheese shreds

Optional: a slice of chopped bacon, cooked

- Salt, kosher & pepper, ground, as desired

Instructions:

Be sure spinach has thawed fully and drain it. Add to mug.

Crack egg into mug. Add cheese, milk and bacon (if you're using). Season as desired. Mix till combined well.

Use a paper towel to cover mug. Microwave on the high setting for three minutes, till cooked fully. Serve and share.

3 – Eggs Lorraine

This is a delicious breakfast, elegant and suitable for special occasions. It's easy to make, too, and can be made, then shared, by you and your date.

Makes 2 Servings

Cooking + Prep Time: 45 minutes

Ingredients:

- 4 slices of bacon, Canadian
- 2 slices of cheese, Swiss
- 4 eggs, large
- 2 tbsp. of sour cream, light
- 1/8 tsp. of salt, kosher
- 1/8 tsp. of pepper, ground

Optional: chives, minced

Instructions:

Preheat the oven to 350F. Coat 2 small oval baking dishes using non-stick spray. Line with the Canadian bacon and top that with cheese. Break 2 eggs in each dish.

In small-sized bowl, whisk the sour cream, kosher salt & ground pepper till smooth. Drop by teaspoons full atop eggs.

Leave dishes uncovered. Bake in 350F oven for 25 to 30 minutes, till eggs have set. Use chives to sprinkle, if desired. Serve and share.

4 – Breakfast Quesadillas for 2

This is an easy recipe for busy mornings together. It's served in a tortilla for ease, and you can add salsa if you like breakfast with a kick.

Makes 2 Servings

Cooking + Prep Time: 40 minutes

Ingredients:

- 4 beaten eggs, large
- 1/2 cup of Mexican cheese blend shreds
- 2 x 7" flour or whole wheat tortillas
- 4 slices of Canadian bacon
- Salsa, as desired

Instructions:

Use 1/4 cup of cheese to sprinkle on each of your tortillas. Top each tortilla with 2 slices of Canadian bacon.

Coat a non-stick, large skillet using cooking spray and heat on med. till hot.

Add eggs. As they start setting, pull eggs gently across pan, forming soft, large curds. Continue to cook while lifting, folding and pulling eggs, stirring only occasionally, until they thicken and no liquid egg is visible.

Spoon the eggs atop Canadian bacon. Fold the tortillas over their fillings and cover by pressing tortillas gently.

Clean the skillet and coat it with non-stick spray. Heat on med-low till it's hot. Toast the quesadillas for 1-2 minutes on each side, just till cheese melts. Cut the wraps into wedges and serve along with salsa, if desired, then share.

5 – Broiled Grapefruit Breakfast

Even if you're not a particular fan of grapefruit, try it this way, and it may win you over. It's delicious and perfect for sharing.

Makes 2 Servings

Cooking + Prep Time: 20 minutes

Ingredients:

- 1 grapefruit, large
- 2 tbsp. of softened butter, unsalted
- 2 tbsp. of sugar, granulated
- 1/2 tsp. of cinnamon, ground

Instructions:

Preheat the broiler.

Cut the grapefruit crossways in halves. Cut around sections and loosen the fruit. Then top with softened butter. Mix the sugar with cinnamon and sprinkle mixture over the fruit.

Place grapefruit on cookie sheet. Broil 4" from the heat till sugar bubbles. Share.

There are so many unique and delightful dishes you can prepare for a date night for 2. Here are some of the best...

6 – Stir Fry Scallops for 2

Mild flavor tomatoes meet scallops in this delicious dish. You can serve it over pasta or rice and use cilantro to garnish, as desired.

Makes 2 Servings

Cooking + Prep Time: 20 minutes

Ingredients:

- 1 chopped onion, small
- 3 minced garlic cloves
- 1 tbsp. of oil, olive
- 3/4 lb. of halved scallops, sea
- 2 chopped plum tomatoes, medium
- 2 tbsp. of lemon juice, fresh
- 1/8 tsp. of pepper, ground

Optional: cooked, hot rice or pasta

Instructions:

In wok or non-stick skillet, stir-fry the garlic and onions in heated oil till they are tender. Add the scallops and stir-fry till they are opaque. Add the tomatoes and stir while cooking for 1 to 2 minutes, till heated fully through.

Stir in ground pepper and fresh lemon juice. Serve for 2 atop rice or pasta, as desired.

7 – Cilantro Sausage with Cauliflower Lime Rice

This simple cauliflower and sausage dinner is good to go in 1/2 hour or less. It cooks all in a single pan, too, so there's not much clean up at all.

Makes 2 Servings

Cooking + Prep Time: 1/2 hour

Ingredients:

- 3-4 Italian sausages, mild
- 1/2 head of riced cauliflower, fresh
- 1 tbsp. of butter, unsalted
- 3 minced garlic cloves
- 1/4 cup of chicken stock, low sodium
- 1 tbsp. of hot sauce, your favorite type
- 2 tbsp. of lime juice, fresh
- Zest from 1/2 fresh lime
- Chopped cilantro, fresh
- 1 tsp. of seasoning, Italian
- Pepper, cracked, as desired

Instructions:

In skillet on med-low, boil 1/4 cup of filtered water. Add the sausages. Cover skillet. Cook, turning occasionally, till sausages are fully cooked. Remove lid. Allow extra water to evaporate while continuing to turn sausages till browned on all sides. Set aside.

Melt the butter in same skillet. Add garlic. Stir occasionally while cooking for 1 minute. Add the cauliflower rice. Toss and coat well. Add stock, lime juice, hot sauce and Italian seasoning. Simmer for 3 to 4 minutes, till sauce has been reduced a little.

Add cilantro and lime zest to cauliflower rice. Stir quickly. Season as desired. Add the sausages back to skillet. Quickly reheat for 1-2 minutes. Serve and share.

8 – Pork Chops & Rhubarb for 2

These tender pork chops have a special taste because of their unique rhubarb sauce. It's rather tangy, so you can add extra honey if you like to sweeten the sauce a little.

Makes 2 Servings

Cooking + Prep Time: 1/2 hour

Ingredients:

- 1 tbsp. of flour, all-purpose
- Kosher salt & ground pepper, as desired
- 2 pork chops from loin, bone-in
- 2 tbsp. of butter, unsalted
- 1/2 lb. of chopped rhubarb, frozen or fresh
- 1 tbsp. of honey, pure
- 1/8 tsp. of cinnamon, ground
- 1 & 1/2 tsp. of minced parsley, fresh

Instructions:

In shallow, wide dish, combine flour, kosher salt & ground pepper. Add the chops and coat by turning.

In medium or large skillet, melt the butter on med. heat. Add the pork chops and cook for 4 to 5 minutes per side, till internal temperature reaches 145F. Remove chops and keep them warm.

Add rhubarb, cinnamon and honey to skillet. Cook for 4-5 minutes, till rhubarb becomes tender. Add sauce over chops and use parsley to sprinkle. Serve and share.

9 – Shrimp & Lettuce Wraps

These wraps offer a wonderful combination of textures and flavors. They include grilled shrimp, carrots, zucchini and sautéed peppers in a crisp leaf of lettuce. The peanut dipping sauce is the final delightful taste.

Makes 2 Servings

Cooking + Prep Time: 25 minutes

Ingredients:

- 1 tbsp. of oil, olive
- 1 lb. of peeled, deveined shrimp, raw
- 1 sliced bell pepper, red
- 2 grated garlic cloves
- 1 diced onion, small
- 1/4 cup of soy sauce, reduced sodium
- 1 tbsp. of ginger, grated
- 1 tsp. of crushed chili pepper, red
- 1/2 tsp. of cumin, ground
- 1 julienned zucchini, fresh
- 1-2 julienned carrots, medium
- 2 seeded, diced jalapeños, fresh
- Chopped chives, fresh
- Salt, kosher, as desired
- Pepper, ground, as desired
- 1 head of lettuce, Boston, butter, Bibb or your favorite type

For dipping: peanut sauce, store-bought

Instructions:

Heat oil in skillet on med-high. Add shrimp. Cook for 2 to 3 minutes, till golden.

Stir in cumin, chili pepper, onions and ginger. Cook for a minute. Add the soy sauce and zucchini and cook for a minute more. Add jalapeño, carrots, bell pepper, chives & garlic. Cook 1 to 2 minutes more. You want vegetables cooked but still with a crunch. Season as desired.

Add a few tbsp. of veggie and shrimp mixture to middle of leaf lettuce as you would with a taco. Serve with remaining juice from cooking, if you like. Use dipping sauce to add extra flavor.

10 – Homemade Taco Salad for 2

This taco salad is the perfect size for two people to share. It's refreshing and light, especially during the warmer months of the year.

Makes 2 Servings

Cooking + Prep Time: 1/2 hour

Ingredients:

- 1/2 lb. of beef, ground
- 1/3 cup of bean dip, store-bought
- 1/4 tsp. of salt, kosher
- 1 tsp. of chili powder
- 1 cup of diced tomatoes, canned + 2 tbsp. tomato liquid from can
- 2 cups of lettuce, chopped
- 1/2 cup of cheddar cheese shreds
- 2 sliced onions, green
- 2 tbsp. of ripe olive slices
- 1/2 cup of corn chips, regular

Instructions:

In large-sized skillet, cook ground beef on med. heat till it has browned and no pink remains, then drain. Add and stir bean dip into beef. Add salt, chili powder & liquid from tomatoes. Remove from heat.

In large mixing bowl, combine tomatoes, cheese, olives, lettuce and onions. Add the beef mixture and toss well. Add chips on top. Serve and share.

11 – Chicken & Spinach with Parmesan Sauce

This recipe for chicken breasts with creamy spinach is a winner for a quick dinner for two. It's made in one pan and doesn't take long for a date night meal.

Makes 2 Servings

Cooking + Prep Time: 1/2 hour

Ingredients:

- 2 chicken breasts
- 3 tbsp. of butter, unsalted
- Kosher salt & cracked pepper, as desired
- 1 minced onion, medium
- 4 minced garlic cloves
- 1 tsp. of oregano
- 1 small-sized jar of tomatoes, sun-dried, drained & chopped – reserve a bit of oil
- 1/2 cup of broth, chicken
- 1/2 cup of cream, heavy
- 1/3 cup of Parmesan cheese, grated
- 1 cup of spinach, fresh

Instructions:

Season the chicken thoroughly on both sides using kosher salt, ground pepper & 1/2 tsp. oregano.

In large-sized skillet, melt 2 tbsp. of butter and a bit of the oil from jarred tomatoes on med-high. Add the chicken breasts. Cook till browned, 4-5 minutes per side. Once no pink remains, transfer chicken to plate. Set it aside.

To prepare the sauce, add last tbsp. of butter to same skillet. Cook garlic, onions, tomatoes and 1/2 tsp. of oregano together. Add broth, cream & Parmesan cheese slowly. Mix, combining till smooth as you simmer the mixture for 2 to 3 minutes. Season as desired.

Add spinach to skillet. Cook till it wilts. Add back chicken to skillet. Reheat it for 2 to 3 minutes. Transfer to platter and use parsley to garnish. Serve and share.

12 – BBQ Tropical Chicken for 2

This is among my favorite date night dinners since it uses a slow cooker. The sauce is delicious and a bit spicy to finish off tasty dishes.

Makes 2 Servings

Cooking + Prep Time: 20 minutes + 3-4 hours slow cooker time

Ingredients:

- 2 leg quarters of chicken – remove skin
- 3 tbsp. of ketchup, no salt added
- 2 tbsp. of orange juice, fresh
- 1 tbsp. of sugar, brown
- 1 tbsp. of vinegar, red wine
- 1 tbsp. of oil, olive
- 1 tsp. of minced parsley, fresh
- 1/2 tsp. of Worcestershire sauce, low sodium
- 1/4 tsp. of salt, garlic
- 1/8 tsp. of pepper, black
- 1 tbsp. of water, cold
- 2 tsp. of corn starch

Instructions:

Cut chicken quarters at joints, as desired. Add to small or medium slow cooker.

In small-sized bowl, combine orange juice, ketchup, vinegar, brown sugar, parsley, oil, Worcestershire sauce, black pepper and garlic salt. Pour mixture over the chicken.

Cover slow cooker. Cook on low setting for 3 to 4 hours, till chicken becomes tender. Remove the chicken to platter and keep it warm.

Skim the fat from your cooking juices and transfer 1/2 cup of it into a small pan. Bring to boil.

Combine water and corn starch till smooth. Stir gradually into pan. Bring to boil and stir while cooking for 2-3 minutes, till it thickens. Serve sauce with the chicken and use parsley to garnish, as desired.

13 – Salmon Teriyaki Bowl

This salmon bowl is packed with flavor and simple to make and share. The salmon will be glazed with teriyaki sauce and served on rice.

Makes 2 Servings

Cooking + Prep Time: 35 minutes

Ingredients:

- 1 pound of chunk-cut salmon filets
- 1 cup of rice, your choice of type
- 3 tbsp. of vinegar, rice
- 1/2 tsp. of salt, kosher
- 1 tbsp. of honey, pure
- 1 tsp. of sugar, brown
- 2 tsp. of tamari sauce or soy sauce
- 1 tsp. of oil, sesame
- 1/2 tsp. of garlic, grated
- 1/2 tsp. of ginger, grated

Optional: 1 tbsp. of hot sauce, as desired

- 4 chopped scallions
- 2 tbsp. of seeds, sesame
- 5 oz. of beans, edamame
- 1 sliced avocado, fresh

Instructions:

Cook rice using directions on the package. Add a bit of butter, as desired.

Mix brown sugar, vinegar and kosher salt together in small-sized bowl. Stir till salt and sugar have dissolved. When rice has cooked, pour dressing over it. Stir to coat the rice with dressing.

Divide hot rice in two bowls. Use sesame seeds for sprinkling. In third bowl, arrange avocado slices and edamame.

In small bowl, mix honey, tamari, sesame oil, ginger, garlic & hot sauce together.

Heat 1 tbsp. of oil in skillet on med. heat. Add salmon chunks. Brown quickly on each side. Pour teriyaki sauce on top.

Raise heat to high. Stir and coat salmon fully in teriyaki sauce. Continue cooking on high while occasionally stirring for 2-3 minutes, till salmon is cooked as you desire and glazed all over. Remove from pan. Scoop onto rice bowls. Serve and share.

14 – Stuffed Bell Peppers for 2

This is a smaller recipe for peppers, making servings just for 2. Most recipes use large quantities. We use a small-sized baking dish, so the peppers don't tip over as they are baking.

Makes 2 Servings

Cooking + Prep Time: 1 & 1/4 hours

Ingredients:

- 2 medium peppers, green
- 1/2 lb. of beef, ground
- 1 x 8-oz. can of tomato sauce, no salt added
- 1/4 cup of instant rice, uncooked
- 3 tbsp. of cheddar cheese shreds
- 1 tbsp. of onion, chopped
- 1/2 tsp. of Worcestershire sauce, low sodium
- 1/2 tsp. of salt, kosher
- 1/4 tsp. of pepper, black
- 1 beaten egg, large

Instructions:

Preheat oven to 350F.

Cut bell pepper tops off. Discard them. Remove the seeds. Blanch the peppers in filtered, boiling water for five minutes. Drain, then rinse using cold water and set peppers aside.

In medium bowl, mix 1/4 cup of tomato sauce, beef, 2 tbsp. of cheese, rice, onions, egg, Worcestershire sauce, kosher salt & black pepper. Combine well.

To stuff peppers, place in casserole dish and fill with mixture from step 2. Pour remainder of tomato sauce over them. Cover dish. Bake in 350F oven for 45 minutes to an hour, till peppers have become tender and meat shows no remaining pink.

Sprinkle peppers using remainder of cheese. Return to 350F oven till cheese melts, 4-5 minutes or so. Serve and share.

15 – Noodle & Spring Roll Salad

This noodle salad is easy to make and wonderful to share. It's perfect for those spring nights when you want a fresh dish.

Makes 2 Servings

Cooking + Prep Time: 25 minutes

Ingredients:

- 1/2 pkg. of noodles, rice
- 2 carrots, medium
- 1/2 sliced cucumber, seedless
- 1 scallion, sliced
- Chopped cilantro, fresh
- 1/2 sliced onion, red
- Honey & ginger dressing, store-bought

Instructions:

Cook the noodles using instructions on package. Strain and rinse using cold water. Set noodles aside.

Cut carrot tops off. Peel carrots. Shred or grate with box grater.

Slice scallion thinly. Discard root end. Then add cucumbers, cilantro, scallion and onions to bowl with the carrots. Drizzle some dressing over mixture and combine by tossing.

Transfer cooked noodles to bowl with carrot mixture. Drizzle with remainder of dressing, or as desired. Stir and combine well. Season as desired, then serve and share.

16 – Steak Salad with Fries for 2

This recipe was modeled after a popular dish created at local restaurants in Pennsylvania. It uses bottled sweet & sour dressing to give it a unique taste.

Makes 2 Servings

Cooking + Prep Time: 25 minutes

Ingredients:

- 1 cup of French fries, frozen
- 1/2 lb. of sirloin steak, beef
- 3 cups of torn lettuce, iceberg
- 1/3 cup of tomato, chopped
- 1/4 cup of chopped onion, red
- 1/2 cup of mozzarella cheese shreds
- Sweet & sour dressing, store-bought

Instructions:

Cook the French fried potatoes using instructions on package.

Coat a skillet with non-stick spray. Place on med. heat. Add the steak and cook for 5 to 6 minutes on each side, till it has reached the doneness level you desire. Remove meat from the heat and allow to sit for 5-10 minutes before you slice it.

Divide lettuce, onions and tomatoes on two plates. Top with steak, potatoes and cheese shreds. Use dressing to drizzle. Serve and share.

17 – Chicken & Dumplings

This recipe was passed down through generations of a family. It makes a wonderful comfort food for date night, with leftovers to use for dinner another night.

Makes 6 Servings

Cooking + Prep Time: 1 hour & 10 minutes

Ingredients:

- Dumplings, prepared

For the Soup

- 2 tbsp. of oil, olive
- 1 chopped onion, large
- 2 peeled, diced carrots, medium
- 1 chopped celery stalk
- 1 tsp. of oregano, dried
- Salt, kosher, as desired
- Pepper, ground, as desired
- 3 minced garlic cloves
- 6 cups of chicken broth, low sodium
- 4 chicken thighs, skinless, boneless
- 2 chicken breasts, skinless, boneless
- 3 thyme sprigs
- 1 cup of cream, heavy

To serve: chopped parsley, fresh

Instructions:

Heat the oil on med. heat in large-sized pot. Add carrots, celery and onions. Cook for 5-6 minutes, till tender. Season as desired. Add the garlic. Cook for a minute, till fragrant.

Add the chicken, broth & thyme to the pot. Bring to boil. Reduce the heat level. Simmer for 10-12 minutes, till chicken has cooked fully through with no pink remaining. Remove the chicken and use two forks to shred it.

Add cream and chicken shreds to the pot. Return to simmer. Drop the dumplings into the pot. Cover pot and cook over low heat for 5-6 minutes, till dumplings have cooked fully through. Use parsley to garnish, then serve and share.

18 – Turkey Stir Fry for 2

Eating healthy sometimes seems boring and bland, but this healthy dish is neither of those. The spiciness makes it a unique dish compared to many turkey recipes.

Makes 2 Servings

Cooking + Prep Time: 35 minutes

Ingredients:

- 2 oz. of noodles, thick rice
- 1/2 lb. of turkey, ground
- 1 chopped onion, small
- 1/2 cup of shredded cabbage, red
- 1/2 cup of chopped kale, fresh
- 1/4 cup of chopped parsley sprigs, fresh
- 1 tsp. of oil, coconut
- 1/2 tsp. of pepper, ground
- 1/4 tsp. of salt, kosher
- 3 thinly sliced onions, green
- 1 sliced pepper, jalapeño
- 2 tsp. of chili sauce, Sriracha

Optional: peanut sauce, Thai-style, bottled

Instructions:

Cook the noodles using instructions on package.

In large, non-stick skillet, cook the turkey, cabbage, kale and onions on med-high for 8 to 10 minutes, crumbling turkey as you go, till turkey has no pink remaining and vegetables have become tender.

Drain the noodles and add them to the skillet. Stir in coconut oil, parsley, ground pepper and kosher salt. Top with chili sauce, jalapeno, green onions and peanut sauce, if using. Serve and share.

19 – Flatbread Veggie Pizza

Using flatbread for pizza saves you the time and trouble of making the dough yourself. Then, you and your date can get down to the business of enjoying this healthy dinner.

Makes 2+ Servings

Cooking + Prep Time: 55 minutes

Ingredients:

- 2 medium flatbreads, prepared

For the Topping

- 12 oz. of halved tomatoes, grape
- 1/4 sliced small onion, red
- 2 tsp. of oil, olive
- 2 tsp. of oregano, chopped
- Salt, kosher, as desired
- Pepper, ground, as desired
- 8 oz. of mozzarella cheese, sliced in 1/4-inch thick circles

To serve:

- Balsamic glaze
- 2 cups of arugula

Instructions:

In medium-sized bowl, combine the oil, onions, tomatoes and oregano. Season as desired.

Top flatbreads with mozzarella and onion-tomato mixture. Bake for 13-15 minutes, till cheese becomes melty. Use balsamic glaze to drizzle, then use arugula to top. Serve and share.

20 – Spicy Enchiladas for 2

Prepared enchilada sauce and pre-cooked strips of chicken bring this recipe to life swiftly. It's a wonderful date night dinner for 2 or can be doubled for the family or guests.

Makes 2 Servings

Cooking + Prep Time: 35 minutes

Ingredients:

- 1 x 6-oz. pkg. of chicken strips, Southwestern-style, ready to use
- 1 & 1/2 cups of cheddar cheese shreds
- 1 x 10-oz. can of enchilada sauce
- 1 cup of beans, refried
- 4 x 7" warmed tortillas, flour
- 1 x 2 & 1/2-oz. can of drained ripe olives, sliced

Optional toppings: shredded lettuce & chopped tomatoes

Instructions:

Preheat oven to 400F.

In large-sized bowl, combine the chicken with 1/2 cup sauce and a cup of shredded cheese. Spread 1/4 cup of beans down middle of tortillas. Top with the chicken mixture and roll them up.

Place enchiladas in 2 small casserole dishes. Top with remainder of sauce & cheese. Use olives to sprinkle.

Cover the baking dishes. Bake for 15 to 20 minutes in 400F oven, till heated fully through. Top with lettuce and tomatoes, if desired. Serve and share.

21 – Creamy Parmesan Tomato Soup

This easy parmesan and tomato soup is a wonderful choice for dates on chilly evenings. You can also add broccoli or kale if you want a heartier meal for 2.

Makes 6 Servings

Cooking + Prep Time: 50 minutes

Ingredients:

- 1 tbsp. of butter, unsalted
- 1/2 diced onion, medium
- 4 minced garlic cloves
- 3 tsp. of seasoning, Italian
- 1/2 tsp. of pepper flakes, red
- 3 tbsp. of flour, all-purpose
- 3 tbsp. of tomato paste, no salt added
- 3 cups of vegetable or chicken broth, low sodium
- 1 x 28-oz. can of tomatoes, diced
- 4 cups of tortellini, cheese
- 1/3 cup of cream, heavy
- 1/2 cup of Parmesan cheese, grated
- 3 cups of packed spinach, fresh
- Salt, kosher, as desired
- Pepper, ground, as desired

For garnish: 2 tbsp. of basil, thinly sliced

Instructions:

In large-sized pot on med. heat, melt the butter. Add the onions. Cook 4-6 minutes, till translucent and soft. Add the garlic. Cook a minute more, till it is fragrant. Add flour, pepper flakes & Italian seasoning and combine by whisking. Cook for a minute longer.

Add the tomato paste. Cook 2-3 minutes, till slightly darkened. Add tomatoes and broth and bring mixture to boil. Lower to simmer. Add tortellini. Cook for 10-12 minutes, till it is cooked through and tender.

Add Parmesan cheese and cream. Stir, combining well. Add the spinach and allow it to wilt. Season as desired and use basil to garnish. Serve and share.

22 – Curried Chicken for 2

Your significant other will love trying new dishes with you, and this one is a winner. Its lively flavor brings out the true flavor of chicken.

Makes 2 Servings

Cooking + Prep Time: 3 hours & 25 minutes

Ingredients:

- 1 sliced onion, small
- 1 tbsp + 1/3 cup of water, filtered
- 1/2 lb. of cubed chicken breast meat, skinless, boneless
- 1 peeled & chopped apple, small
- 1/4 cup of raisins, golden or dark
- 1 tsp. of curry powder
- 1 minced garlic clove
- 1/4 tsp. of ginger, ground
- 1/8 tsp. of salt, kosher
- 1 & 1/2 tsp. of flour, all-purpose
- 1 tsp. of bouillon granules, chicken
- 1/2 cup of sour cream, light
- 3/4 tsp. of corn starch
- 1 tbsp. of green onions, sliced thinly
- Cooked rice, hot

Instructions:

Place 1 tbsp. of water and onions in glass bowl. Cover. Microwave using high setting for 1 - 1 & 1/2 minutes, till tender but crisp.

In a small slow cooker, combine chicken, raisins, apple, curry, garlic, ginger, onion and salt.

Combine remainder of water with flour and bouillon. Pour this over the chicken mixture. Cover. Cook on the low setting for 3 – 3 & 1/2 hours till juices from chicken are running clear and no pink remains.

Transfer chicken mixture to medium bowl and keep it warm. Transfer juices to small pan. Combine sour cream at room temperature with corn starch till you have a smooth mixture. Add it to the juices. Stir while cooking on med. heat till it thickens. Pour over the chicken mixture and coat by tossing. Use green onions to sprinkle. Serve along with rice and share.

23 – Asparagus & Lemon Chicken Pasta

This is a fresh and tasty pasta that will remind you of spring. It's a great dish to share together on date night too.

Makes 4 Servings

Cooking + Prep Time: 35 minutes

Ingredients:

- Salt, kosher
- 1 pound of spaghetti or linguine
- 1 tbsp. of oil, olive
- 1 pound of chicken breasts, skinless, boneless
- Pepper, ground, as desired
- 2 tsp. of seasoning, Italian
- 2 tbsp. of butter, unsalted
- 1 chopped small onion, red
- 1 pound of asparagus – trim the stalks
- 3/4 cup of cream, heavy
- 1/2 cup of chicken broth, low sodium
- 1 fresh lemon, juice
- 1 half-moon sliced lemon, fresh
- 3 minced garlic cloves
- 3/4 cup of mozzarella shreds
- 1/2 cup of Parmesan, grated, + extra for garnishing

To garnish: chopped parsley, fresh

Instructions:

Cook the pasta using instructions on package. Drain, then return it to the pot.

Heat the oil in skillet on med. heat. Add the chicken. Add Italian seasoning, kosher salt & ground pepper. Cook for 8-9 minutes each side, till golden, with no pink remaining. Transfer to plate and allow to rest before slicing thinly.

Melt the butter on med. heat in skillet. Add asparagus and red onions. Season as desired. Cook for 4-5 minutes, till tender. Add broth, cream, lemon juice & garlic. Simmer for 5-7 minutes.

Stir in the cheese. Allow mixture to cook till cheese is melty. Add linguine and lemon slices. Top with chicken slices. Use parmesan & parsley to garnish. Serve and share.

24 – Tilapia for 2

This is a simple healthy dinner that you and your date will both enjoy. The tilapia and spices deliver a wonderful boost of flavor.

Makes 2 Servings

Cooking + Prep Time: 1/2 hour

Ingredients:

- 2 x 6-oz. fillets, tilapia
- 1 melted tbsp. of butter, unsalted
- 1 tsp. of steak seasoning, Montreal or similar
- 1/2 tsp. of parsley flakes, dried
- 1/4 tsp. of paprika, sweet
- 1/4 tsp. of thyme, dried
- 1/8 tsp. of salt, kosher
- 1/8 tsp. of pepper, ground
- 1/8 tsp. of onion powder
- 1 dash of garlic powder seasoning

Instructions:

Preheat the oven to 425F.

Place the tilapia fillets in lightly greased 11" x 7" casserole dish. Drizzle them with unsalted butter.

In small-sized bowl, mix the remainder of ingredients and sprinkle mixture over the fillets.

Cover dish and bake in 425F oven for 8-10 minutes. Remove cover. Bake for 6-8 minutes, till fish starts flaking easily when you use a fork. Serve and share.

25 – Sage & Lemon Ricotta Gnudi

You and your date will enjoy gnudi, which are simply a light version of the better-known gnocchi. It's made with ricotta rather than potatoes, creating a tasty and unique dish.

Makes 6 Servings

Cooking + Prep Time: 1 & 1/4 hours + 1 hour chilling time

Ingredients:

- 1 lb. of drained ricotta, fresh
- 1 cup of finely grated parmesan cheese
- 2/3 cup of sifted flour, plain
- 1/3 cup of semolina, fine, + extra for dusting
- 2 tbsp. of sage, chopped + extra leaves for frying
- 2 lightly beaten eggs, large
- 1 pinch of nutmeg, ground
- 1 tsp. of salt, flaked
- 1 fresh lemon, grated zest
- 1/2 to 1 lemon, juice, freshy squeezed
- 1/2 cup of oil, olive
- 1 & 3/4 oz. of chopped butter, unsalted
- 1/2 finely chopped garlic clove

For serving: parmesan, grated

Instructions:

Add parmesan, ricotta, semolina, flour, eggs, sage, lemon zest, nutmeg & 1 tsp. flaked salt in large bowl. Gently mix.

Work mixture in 24 egg-shaped dumplings. Then dust cookie sheet with semolina. Place the dumplings on sheet in one layer. Leave uncovered and place in refrigerator to chill for an hour or longer.

Heat 1/2 oil in large frying pan on med-high. Add 1/2 of gnudi dumplings. Turn carefully while cooking till outsides are crispy and golden, 4 to 5 minutes. Remove from pan. Place on separate tray & keep them warm. Repeat with remainder of oil and gnudi dumplings.

Add sage leaves into pan. Fry in the leftover oil till crisp, about 10 seconds. Remove leaves and set them aside.

Add butter, fresh lemon juice & garlic to pan. Simmer till garlic turns golden and butter becomes nutty, 2 to 3 minutes. Drizzle the gnudi dumplings with fresh lemon sauce. Top them with the fried sage. Scatter grated parmesan on top. Serve and share

End your evening date for 2 with a dessert specially made for 2...

26 – Crème Brulee with White Chocolate

For special occasions and dinner dates, this is a perfect dessert choice. It's written to be prepared for 2 and by 2 if you like.

Makes 2 Servings

Cooking + Prep Time: 1 hour & 10 minutes + 4 hours refrigeration time

Ingredients:

- 3 yolks from large eggs
- 6 tbsp. of sugar, granulated
- 1 cup of whipping cream, heavy
- 2 oz. of finely chopped baking chocolate, white
- 1/4 tsp. of vanilla extract, pure

Instructions:

In small-sized bowl, whisk the egg yolks with 2 tbsp. of sugar. Set them aside.

In small pan, combine chocolate, cream and 2 more tbsp. of sugar. Heat on med-low while constantly stirring till mixture smooths out and chocolate melts.

Remove mixture from heat and stir in the vanilla. Stir a bit of heated filling into yolk mixture. Return everything to pan and stir constantly.

Pour mixture into 2 x 10-oz. ramekins and place them on a rimmed casserole dish. Add an inch boiling water to the casserole dish.

Leave ramekins uncovered and bake in 325F oven till centers have set, 50 to 55 minutes. Remove ramekins from the water bath. Allow to cool for 10-12 minutes. Place in refrigerator for 4 hours or longer.

Sprinkle with the remainder of sugar. Heat the sugar with crème brulee torch till sugar caramelizes. Share promptly.

27 – Strawberries Romanov for 2

This is an elegant but quick dessert made with a cream sauce with fresh strawberries. It looks almost as good as it will taste.

Makes 2 Servings

Cooking + Prep Time: 40 minutes

Ingredients:

- 1/2 cup of sour cream, light
- 1 & 1/2 cups of softened ice cream, vanilla
- 1 cup of whipped cream, sweetened
- 1/4 cup of liqueur, orange, +/- as desired
- 2 cups of hulled strawberries, fresh

To garnish: 2 mint leaves

To garnish: semi-sweet chocolate, shaved

Instructions:

In medium-sized bowl, stir sour cream, whipped cream and ice cream together.

Stir in orange liqueur gradually. Divide berries into 2 parfait glasses. Spoon cream mixture atop berries. Use mint leaves & shaved chocolate to garnish. Serve and share.

28 – Turtle Cheesecake for 2

This rich cheesecake dish is easy to whip up. It has the layers of chocolate, vanilla and caramel, and it's fun to share.

Makes 2 Servings

Cooking + Prep Time: 45 minutes + 8 hours refrigeration time

Ingredients:

- 1/3 cup of vanilla wafers, crushed
- 4 tsp. of melted butter, unsalted
- 4 oz. of softened cream cheese, light
- 2 tbsp. of sugar, granulated
- 1/2 tsp. of vanilla extract, pure
- 2 tbsp. of room temp. egg, beaten
- 2 tbsp. of ice cream topping, hot fudge flavor, warmed up
- 3 tbsp. of ice cream topping, hot caramel

Instructions:

Preheat oven to 350F.

In small-sized bowl, combine butter with wafer crumbs. Press into bottom and a half-inch up sides of lightly greased 4-inch springform-type pan.

In separate bowl, beat cream cheese, vanilla and sugar till smooth. Add the eggs. Beat at low speed till barely combined. Spread 1/2 of this mixture in crust. Stir the fudge topping into remainder of batter. Spread gently over the layer of cream cheese. Place the pan on cookie sheet.

Bake in 350F oven for 20 to 25 minutes, till middle is nearly set. Cool for 8-10 minutes on wire rack. Run knife carefully around pan edge to loosen and allow to cool for one hour more.

Place in the refrigerator overnight and remove the sides of springform pan. Drizzle the caramel topping atop cheesecake. Serve.

29 – Bananas Foster

This is a simple dessert to make, but it's a show-stopping dessert for you and that special someone. It does not include too many ingredients and does only take minutes to prepare.

Makes 2 Servings

Cooking + Prep Time: 20 minutes

Ingredients:

- 3 tbsp. of butter, unsalted
- 3 tbsp. of brown sugar, packed
- 2 peeled bananas, peeled & halved lengthways, then crossways
- 2 fl. oz. of rum
- 1 fl. oz. of liqueur, banana
- 2 pinches of cinnamon, ground
- 2 scoops of ice cream, vanilla
- 2 mint sprigs, small

Instructions:

Melt brown sugar into butter in skillet on med-high for 3-5 minutes, till butter has melted and mixture is starting to bubble.

Place the bananas with cut side facing down in the brown sugar mixture. Cook for 1/2 minute or so, till barely golden. Flip, then cook for another 1/2 minute so other side can cook.

Remove skillet from the heat. Pour the rum & banana liqueur in skillet. Put skillet back on high heat. Cook till the alcohol has ignited and flamed, 1-3 minutes, then add the cinnamon. When the flames have died down, remove skillet from heat again.

Scoop ice cream in two bowls. Divide banana mixture in the bowls. Use mint sprigs to garnish. Serve and share.

30 – Coconut Pie with Meringue for 2

This mini coconut pie features a fluffy filling or meringue that bakes up beautifully. It's sprinkled with the toasted flakes of coconut.

Makes 2 Servings

Cooking + Prep Time: 1 hour & 5 minutes + 3 hours & 15 minutes refrigeration time

Ingredients:

- 1/2 cup of flour, all-purpose
- 1/8 tsp. of salt, kosher
- 2 tbsp. of water, cold
- 2 tbsp. of shortening

For the Filling

- 3 tbsp. of sugar, granulated
- 1 cup of milk, 2%
- 4 & 1/2 tsp. of corn starch
- 2 yolks from large eggs
- 3 tbsp. of shredded coconut, sweetened
- 1 tbsp. of butter, unsalted

For the Meringue

- 1 white from large egg
- 1/8 tsp. of cream 'o tartar
- 2 tbsp. of sugar, granulated

Optional: toasted coconut, shredded, sweetened

Instructions:

Preheat oven to 450F.

In small-sized bowl, combine the flour and kosher salt. Cut the shortening in till it has a crumbly texture. Add water gradually while using a fork to toss dough till it has formed a ball shape. Cover. Place in refrigerator for 13-15 minutes, till easy to handle.

Flour your work surface lightly. Roll dough out so it fits a five inch pie plate. Transfer dough to a pie plate. Trim to fit plate plus 1/2" beyond plate edge. Flute the edges. Line crust with 2x thickness of foil.

Bake in 450F oven for 5-7 minutes. Remove the foil and bake for 5 more minutes. Cool on wire rack.

In small pan, combine milk, corn starch, sugar & yolks. Stir while cooking on med. heat till mixture is 160F. Remove from heat. Gently add and stir butter and coconut. Pour filling into the crust.

To prepare the meringue, beat large egg white & cream o' tartar over med, speed till it forms soft peaks. Beat in sugar gradually, 1 tbsp. after another on the high setting till it forms glossy, stiff peaks and sugar has dissolved. Then spread meringue over the heated filling and seal the edges of crust.

Reduce oven temp to 350F and bake at that temperature for 10 to 15 minutes, till golden brown. Cool on wire rack for 1/2 hour. Place in refrigerator for 3 hours or longer. Use extra shredded coconut to garnish. Serve and share.

Conclusion

This Date Night for 2 cookbook has shown you...

How to use different ingredients to affect unique warming tastes in dishes for two.

How can you include date night recipes in your home repertoire?

You can...

Make eggs Lorraine and coconut lime smoothie bowls, which you may not have tried before. They are just as mouthwatering tasty as they sound.

Cook soups and stews, comfort food for date night. Find their ingredients in meat & produce or frozen food sections of your local grocery stores.

Enjoy making the delectable seafood date night dishes, including salmon and tilapia. Fish is a mainstay in the recipes, and there are SO many ways to make it great.

Make dishes using potatoes and pasta in dinners for 2. There is something about these ingredients that makes the dishes more comforting.

Make desserts like turtle cheesecake and strawberries Romanov for 2. They are tasty and tempting for your date.

Share the special recipes with your date!

Author Biography

Growing up with parents from different cultures, who had different traditions gave Rose Rivera a chance to taste the cuisines of two different worlds. Her first step in the cooking career was when she started combining ingredients from dishes from different cuisines.

At that time, she ended up with creations that she couldn't believe. Her mom and dad, and everyone else in the family was surprised about her cooking skills, which gave her even more strength and determination to continue cooking and pursue school and career.

Now Rose is trying to reach everyone in the world through food. Whether it's about classic or innovating recipes, people who got her cookbooks never had a hard time following her instructions. It made things better for them, even for those who weren't spending a lot of time in the kitchen.

Inspired by culture and tradition Rose reached the stars. But she is not stopping anytime soon. She believes that there is no end in cooking and she will continue to cook and create recipes as long as she could.

She says, "Don't be afraid to mix it up sometimes, you never know what you will end up with, maybe your own signature dish. Well, that's it all started for me."

So, you defiantly won't be disappointed with her cookbooks. Once you try out the recipes from one of her books you would like to see all of them.

Thank You!

thank you

This won't be my last book, in fact, there are many books coming soon. So, thank you for getting this book because you will see with your own eyes, smell, and taste that my recipes are worth buying. Your cooking skills will get better and you will have different dishes to serve daily.

I appreciate you for choosing my work, I know you won't be disappointed. Now it's time to try out the recipes and share your experience. Leave feedback so that not only others will know about it but also, I'll be able to become even better in my work, every feedback is welcomed.

Thank you once more for choosing my book

Have an amazing day

Rose Rivera

Printed in Great Britain
by Amazon

85498069R00047